# GET OFF YOUR A$$ AND MANAGE YOUR MONEY

# GET OFF YOUR A$$

# AND MANAGE YOUR MONEY

## Why You Need
## Alternative Investments

CHRIS ODEGARD

# Download The Free Action Guide

Reading a book is one thing; converting the newfound knowledge into *effective action* is something else altogether. I don't want you just to read this book and say, "That was interesting," and walk away. I want you to take your new knowledge and do something with it; create a better financial future for you and your family. To that end, I've created a free action guide, which will move you step-by-step from conventional investments to alternatives efficiently and with fewer mistakes.

Enter the URL below into your browser and enter the password to download your free action guide.

http://theprolificinvestor.net/action-guide/

Password: **Ca$hflow**

## Dedication

*To all of you who aren't where you want to be financially, you can walk a different path than the one on which you find yourself. You can do better, and I want to help. I want to show you the world of alternative investments and why you desperately need them in your portfolio.*

Work hard at your job, and you can make a living. Work hard on yourself, and you can make a fortune.

—Jim Rohn

# Acknowledgment

To my partner, Marnye Moore, who read every word of this book almost as many times as I did and provided valuable insight and feedback; you were instrumental in the writing of this book, and thankfully our relationship survived the endeavor. Many thanks to Tom Creighton and Dr. Ian Kurth, who gave me their honest and sometimes brutal feedback on the book's initial drafts, which sent me back to the drawing board for painful but necessary rewrites. Editor Amy Pattee Colvin and formatter Lucy Holtsnider, you turned this first-time author's words, ideas, and pictures into a thing of professionalism and beauty. The final version of the Hierarchy of Investors, the book's centerpiece, would not be what it is today without the wisdom and guidance of Rod Zabriskie from Money Insights. I am honored that superstar, alternative investor Dave Zook agreed and took the time to write the foreword for this book. And finally, this entire project was initiated by my former business coach, Alana Wopart, who simply asked me if I could write a book, and I said yes!

Numerous people have said in different ways that success is not measured by what you achieve at the end of the journey but by the person you become along the way. Ergo, notwithstanding how the marketplace judges the value of this work, I have grown immeasurably through the process.

# Foreword

I came up with this quote and later trademarked it "You can be conventional, or you can be wealthy, pick one."

I find it interesting that we live in a time where *real assets* are considered alternative assets in the investment world.

In fact, mainstream, conventional, or traditional assets are now considered by many to be paper assets—like stocks, bonds, and mutual funds. Whereas real estate, which is older than dirt—wait, it is dirt—is considered alternative and often risky.

One definition for alternative is "available as another possibility." Really??

So the world we live in considers real assets "alternative" and paper assets as the real thing and where the financial professionals encourage you to place most of your liquid net worth.

As Chris discusses in this book, the concept of investing in real assets is one to which I fully subscribe and have been teaching for more than a decade.

One of the best things about investing in real assets is, many times—when done strategically—you can make lots of tax-free income. The best part is it's tax-free because the government encourages investment in that space.

While conventional wisdom says, "if you make a lot of money, you have to pay a lot of tax," real asset investors believe in taking a non-conventional approach to investing and use the tax law to their advantage—all while helping our government achieve its goals and objectives.

I grew up in a family where I was taught the philosophy, "if you make a lot of money, you have to pay a lot of tax." However, by doing deep dive diligence, getting around some really good folks, and building a great team of advisors, I was able to bypass that way of thinking and move onto the path I travel today and have followed for the last decade.

I believe one of the significant steps in building wealth is to start managing your tax liability, and it's not all that difficult if you have a good team and you get strategic by investing in some carefully selected real assets that will deliver bonus depreciation.

Chris talks about what he has done to build wealth, and I always like to take advice from people who have figured it out and have done it!

To all of you who are convinced there's a better way than what the conventional folks are telling you, there is!

Building tax-free wealth is within your reach if you go after it; seek, and ye shall find.

Go build lots of tax-free wealth and make an impact in your family, your community, and the world around you.

To your success!

The Real Asset Investor

Dave Zook

# Table of Contents

# INTRODUCTION

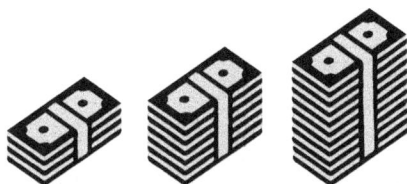

I wasn't always The Prolific Investor. I was raised in a middle-class family in Forest Park, Ohio, a suburb of Cincinnati. Growing up, I learned precisely what my parents knew—get an education, get a job with benefits and a pension, and invest your money in a well-diversified portfolio of stocks, bonds, mutual funds, and ETFs through a 401K.

That's exactly what I did for the next twenty-plus years. I acquired an education at Embry-Riddle Aeronautical University in Daytona Beach, Florida, then went on to work for The Boeing Company. On balance, the more than thirty-three years I spent at Boeing were remarkable, a tremendous adventure and learning experience.

I've traveled to over thirty countries—including Nepal, with a visit to Katmandu. How many people can say they've been to Katmandu?

Over the years, I've had many different jobs—most notable was Director of Contracts, where I wrote and negotiated contracts for the sale of 737, 747, 777, and 787 aircraft to airlines worldwide and one royal family. This is where my love for business was born.

While my formal education stopped with my bachelor's degree from Embry-Riddle, my Boeing Contracts job was an MBA on steroids! What I learned in big business has helped me tremendously in the small business world in which I operate today.

My traditional education and career path served me quite well in many ways. It put me in the middle class, where I raised a family, put two children through college, and I was on track for a comfortable retirement at age sixty-five. I was precisely what Robert Kiyosaki calls an "E"—an employee—in his book *Rich Dad's Cashflow Quadrant: Rich Dad's Guide to Financial Freedom.* Even though being an "E" and following the conventional investing wisdom worked for me to an extent, I now know that I left *millions* of dollars on the table while following that path.

Circumstances are different now than they were for me and my parents' generation. I don't believe the conventional path will work well for my children and other young people today. They will need to be smarter at a younger age than I was. I'll share some startling statistics in support of this in Chapter 3.

The conventional financial path I traveled veered abruptly in 2009 when I experienced a life event where I lost 55 percent of my assets and thousands of dollars per month in cash flow—the life event was a divorce.

After feeling sorry for myself for a while, I picked up a book that sat unread on my nightstand for far too long. The book was *Rich Dad Poor Dad: What The Rich Teach Their Kids About Money – That The Poor And Middle Class Do Not!* by Robert Kiyosaki. The book introduced me to a different way of thinking about money, taxes, and investing.

It launched me on a path of investing almost entirely in alternative investments, sometimes referred to as alternatives. At the time, the term alternative investments wasn't yet embedded in my lexicon as it is today, but I was hooked nonetheless and invested in just about anything unconventional.

In 2018, nine short years after beginning my alternative-investing journey, my financial path was radically different than what I once imagined it would be. I was preparing to retire from Boeing. Who would have thought that just nine years after losing 55 percent of my assets, I'd be retiring at 56, nine years earlier than initially planned? Moving away from conventional financial wisdom was an amazing journey, and I wanted to tell the world about it so that others might do the same.

To that end, I created an avatar, The Prolific Investor, secured TheProlificInvestor.net, and began taking weekly, private, online instruction on how to use WordPress. Over about three months, I built the website and published my first article on November 23, 2018, titled *Is it a Good Idea to Pay off Your Home Mortgage*.

While building the website and writing the content for the various pages, I began to ask myself, why should anyone listen to me? What credentials do I have to write about personal finance and alternative investments? I had a balance sheet and knew my net worth. I have a bookkeeper who provides quarterly financials on all my entities. If only I had a balance sheet from 2009 after the divorce with which to compare. Unfortunately, I wasn't that sophisticated back then and didn't have a balance sheet or those kinds of details.

Then, a flash of brilliance struck me; I did have a balance sheet from 2009! An accounting was required to split our assets 55/45. Sure enough, I dug back into my divorce records and found precisely what our net worth was in 2009. Comparing the balance sheet of 2009 to 2018, I found that even though I lost 55 percent of my assets in 2009, in the nine short years to 2018, I recouped my losses and added *millions* of dollars to it!

Additionally, at the end of 2018, I retired from my corporate job at fifty-six and never need to work again unless I choose to. For younger people, the great news for you is if you start this journey earlier than I did, you can retire at forty-six or thirty-six instead of fifty-six.

Even with that data, is this a success story? Was it a successful decade? It depends. One of the principles in the book *177 Mental Toughness Secrets of the World Class: The Thought Processes, Habits, and Philosophies of the Great Ones* by Steve Siebold, is that champions embrace relativity. Champions ask the question, "Compared to what?"

If I gave the exact numbers to one of my mentors, George Antone, he would ask, "Is that all you accomplished in nine years?" Many others would consider it an amazing success. I'm happy with the results. However, I continue to learn, invest, and improve. Most importantly, I want to help you do the same. This book, along with my blog and videos, are your new tools.

Now that I've told you who I am, I need to tell you who I am not; I am not a financial adviser, financial planner, stock-broker, CPA, or attorney. As such, I can't give you financial, legal, or investment advice. What I can do is share my experiences, successes, and failures with you so that you can blaze your own path and consult with the appropriate professionals of your choosing as you see fit.

While there's a good legal reason for that disclaimer, I offer it more to reinforce that this book is just the tip of the iceberg; it is a small introduction to alternative investments and their many benefits. Entire books have been written on chapters or even subchapters of this book; tax efficiency and asset protection are two examples. Inevitably, in my high-level explanations of some of these topics, I'll get something wrong, so again, consult a professional when it's time to pull the trigger on something. I've listed the advisors I use on the resources page at TheProlificInvestor.net.

# CHAPTER 1

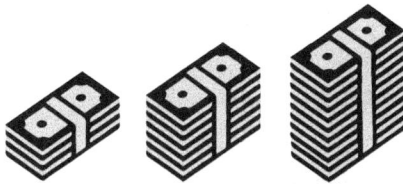

# Maslow's Hierarchy of Needs

During your school years, you may have learned a theory on human motivation called Maslow's Hierarchy of Needs. This theory was first put forth by American psychologist Abraham Maslow in 1943 in *Psychological Review* and later expanded upon in Maslow's 1954 book, *Motivation and Personality*.

It is represented visually in Figure 1, and the diagram shows how humans progress up the hierarchy from bottom to top. First, basic needs are satisfied, and then more advanced needs are met until a person finally reaches self-actualization at the top. From bottom to top, the need categories are as follows:

- Physiological
- Safety
- Belonging and Love
- Esteem
- Self-actualization

Only when the needs at the bottom of the hierarchy are satisfied can humans move up to the next level, and so on.

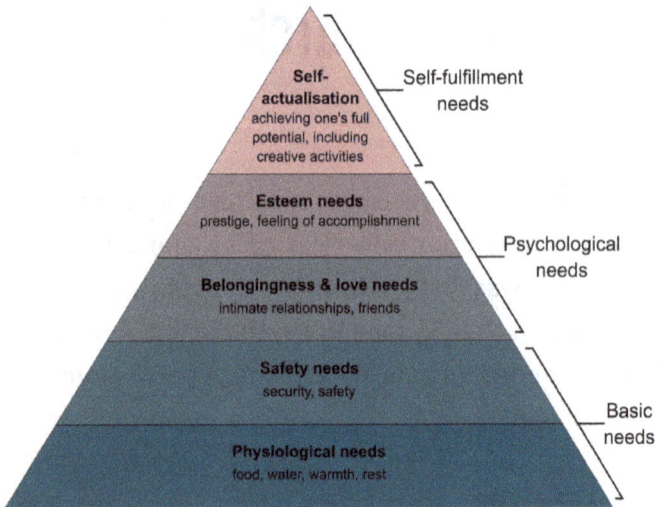

**Figure 1: Maslow's Hierarchy of Needs**

# CHAPTER 2

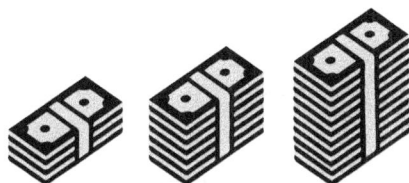

# The Prolific Investor's Hierarchy of Investors

In 2020, I created the Hierarchy of Investors to explain the mission of my alternative investment blog at TheProlific-Investor.net. I wanted to challenge conventional wisdom and move investors up the hierarchy from conventional investments to alternative investments. One big difference between my hierarchy and Maslow's is that you don't have to start at the bottom and work your way up. In my experience, however, that is how most people do it.

## Conventional and Alternative Investments

The Hierarchy of Investors or Pyramid—I will use hierarchy and pyramid interchangeably in this book—is divided into two main categories:

- Those who invest in conventional investments
- Those who invest in alternative investments

The way I've depicted it, conventional investments aren't even on the pyramid; they're in the shadow of the pyramid, in the dark. You only get all the good stuff when you actually get on the pyramid and start climbing.

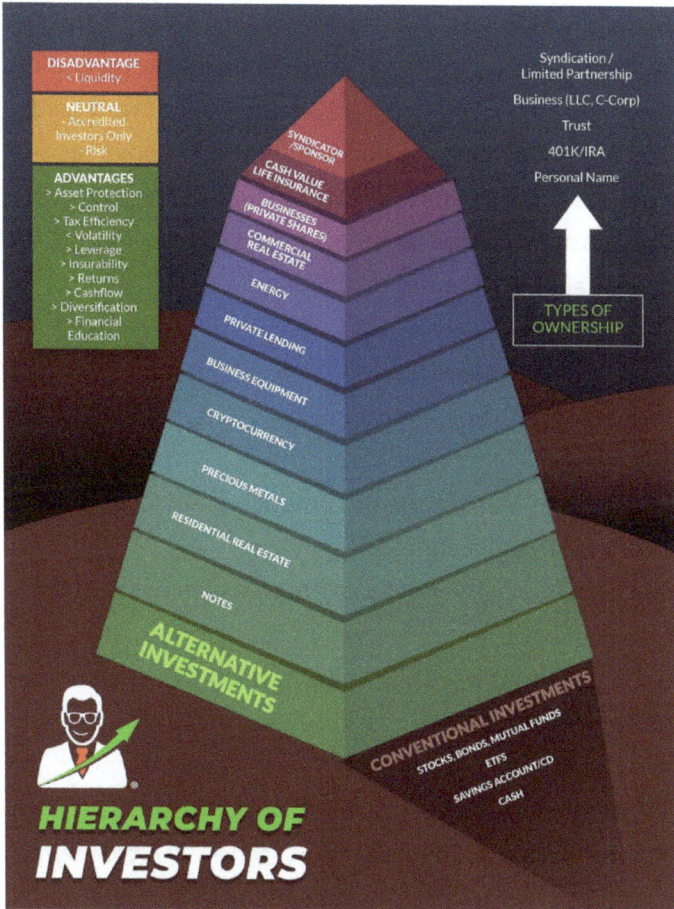

**Figure 2: The Hierarchy of Investors**

Downloadable at https://theprolificinvestor.net/resources/

Being on the conventional investments level of the Hierarchy of Investors is like being on the first level of Maslow's Hierarchy of Needs. You are not meant to stay on the first level; you are meant to move up to the next level and the next, and so on. You don't get a ladder out of your garage and place it against the house to never go above the first rung. It's a ladder; you're meant to climb it. The sad truth is that most Americans never leave the first level despite the overwhelming advantages of doing so.

Besides being divided between conventional and alternative investments, the pyramid shows:

- Examples of investments comprising conventional and alternative investments
- The advantages and disadvantages of moving up the hierarchy
- The different ways of owning investments as you move up the pyramid

So, what are these magical alternative investments? They include but are not limited to:

- Notes
- Residential Real Estate
- Precious Metals
- Cryptocurrency

- Business Equipment
- Private Lending
- Energy
- Commercial Real Estate
- Private Shares of Small Businesses
- Cash Value Life Insurance
- Syndicator/Sponsor

Note: For the remainder of the book, I will use the terms investment and asset interchangeably—thus, a mutual fund can be called an investment or an asset.

# CHAPTER 3

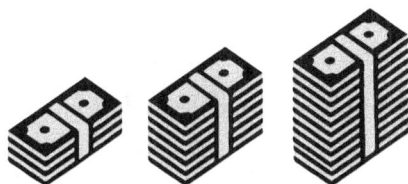

# Conventional Wisdom

The vast majority of Americans follow what I consider conventional wisdom regarding money, investing, and personal financing. They invest in a well-diversified portfolio of stocks, bonds, mutual funds, and exchange-traded funds (ETFs) via a 401K or IRA, all of which fall under the larger umbrella of conventional investments.

So, what's wrong with this strategy? Very simply, it isn't working for most Americans.

According to a study conducted by GoBankingRates.com in 2020 (Anderson, Joel. "How Do Your Finances Measure Up To the Typical American's?" GO BankingRates, 5 June 2020, www.gobankingrates. com/money/financial-planning/average-american-financial-statistics.):

- 34% of Americans have $0 in savings
- 69% of Americans have less than $10K in saving
- 46% of Americans have $0 in retirement savings
- 65% of Americans have less than $10K in retirement savings
- 49% of Americans are living paycheck to paycheck
- 36% of Americans believe they are ready for retirement

According to Investopedia, the S&P 500 Index's average annual return since its inception in 1926 has been 9.8 percent ("S&P 500." Wikipedia The Free Encyclopedia, 5 Oct. 2021, en.wikipedia. org/wiki/S%26P_500.). According to The Balance, the average equity fund investor only earned 5.19 percent annually (Anspach, Dana. "Why Average Investors Earn Below Average Market Returns." The Balance, 26 Mar. 2021, www.thebalance.com/why-average-investors-earn-below-average-market-returns-2388519.). Think about that, a measly 5.19 percent! And that's before inflation and taxes!

Not a very bright picture. If the conventional wisdom were working, we wouldn't have statistics like these.

If conventional wisdom and conventional investments perform so poorly, why do so many people invest in them? I believe there are three reasons, two of which are closely linked.

## It's All We Know

Thanks to massive advertising and no financial education in the school system, conventional wisdom is all we know. We are bombarded with advertisements from financial planners, advisers, brokers, and fund managers who want to help us build a well-diversified portfolio of stocks, bonds, mutual funds, and ETFs. This is then reinforced by our family, friends, and colleagues.

To illustrate this point, I began taking classes on real estate after my divorce, and shortly after that, I asked my seventeen-year-old son to join me in some of these classes. Like me, he was excited about what he was learning and, at the same time, dumbfounded at why he had never heard any of this information before. On the drive home one evening, as we were both excitedly reviewing the day, I told him he could tell anyone he wanted about what he had learned that day but that most people, including some family members, wouldn't share his enthusiasm.

As I predicted, certain family members rained on his parade, telling him what he learned wasn't possible, couldn't be true, or might even be unethical or illegal. Thankfully, my son was not deterred by his adult family members, but you could see how many might just stop at this point and go with the opinion of the people they know, love, and trust.

It's ludicrous when you think about it; conventional investors who were not multi-millionaires telling a seventeen-year-old high school student that he shouldn't invest in real estate. It would be like getting legal advice from your uncle, the landscaper.

To be clear, information about alternative investments is out there, but you have to go look for it because it's not mainstream. You won't hear about alternatives on your local television or radio station or the likes of CNN, FOX, or MSNBC. I hear about alternatives every day on podcasts geared toward entrepreneurs, small business people, and, yes, alternative investors.

### It's Easy

In addition to being the target of advertising our entire lives, the path of conventional wisdom is easy. It takes no financial education to buy a stock, mutual fund, ETF or turn your money over to a financial advisor. In less than thirty minutes, you can set up a brokerage account online and begin buying paper assets, despite not having a clue what you're doing. If your company offers a 401K, it might even auto-enroll you in its 401K, selecting both the amount deducted from each paycheck and the mix of mutual funds in which you'll be investing. Try going to a bank to get a small apartment building loan with no financial education; the bank will send you back to the drawing board!

## There's Money In It—For Other People

There is a massive amount of money to be made in fees by mutual fund managers, brokers, financial advisors, and planners. So much so that they can afford the continual advertising we see and hear daily.

While fees exist in the alternative investment space for sure, the fees that go to the syndicators/sponsors—the equivalent of the fund manager—are typically aligned with the investor. The sponsors don't earn their fees until the investors make money. In some cases, the syndicator doesn't make any money until the investor has received all her original investment back. With conventional investments, advisors and managers make money, *even if you lose money*!

For a more in-depth discussion on this topic, check out *Blog #15 – Alignment Within Your Investments* at TheProlificInvestor.net.

Try going to a financial planner or adviser and tell them you want to include alternative investments in your portfolio. You'll be hard-pressed to find one who will recommend or advise you on this asset class. I have *never* come across a financial planner or advisor who would provide guidance on alternatives. I asked a friend of mine who is a conventional financial advisor why this is the case, and he said there were two reasons:

- Conventional investments provide an easy and automated source of revenue for planners and advisors.
- Advisors can be sued if a client loses money with an alternative investment. This is not the case with conventional investments.

It's hard for me to paint a picture of how badly conventional wisdom damages your finances, your future, and your plans of someday retiring or being financially free. Someone who has done the research and put pen to paper on this topic is Andy Tanner in his book *401(k)aos: How Our Dream of Retirement Became a Nightmare of Chaos.* I highly suggest you read it.

# CHAPTER 4

# An Alternative Investment Example—Automated Teller Machines (ATMs)

Before I launch into the advantages and disadvantages of alternative investments versus conventional investments, let me give you a real-life example of one of my alternative investments, ATMs. I'll refer back to this example throughout the rest of the book. ATMs fall under the real assets category—business equipment—on the hierarchy. While I invest in numerous types of alternatives, I picked

ATMs as my example because the math is the simplest in that they provide a fixed monthly return.

Before I get into the specifics of my ATM investments, here's a general overview of the business. According to a 2019 article in PR Newswire, the ATM market in 2018 was valued at $18.5B ("Global $28.2 Billion ATM Market Analysis & Forecasts to 2024 by Solution, Screen Size, Application, ATM Type, Region." PR Newswire, 23 Aug. 2019, www.prnewswire.com/news-releases/global-28-2-billion-atm-market-analysis--forecasts-to-2024-by-solution-screen-size-application-atm-type-region-300906301.html#:~:text=The%20global%20ATM%20(Automated%20Teller,7%25%20during%202019%2D2024.). Three primary players exist in the ATM space—the location owner (the convenience store owner, for example), the ATM owner/investor (the bank or me in this case), and the management company that locates, operates, and maintains the ATMs. All parties receive a portion of the fees charged to the ATM users, which average around $2.50 per transaction. The management company receives approximately 45 percent, the location owner 25 percent, and the owner/investor 30 percent. Additional revenue may also be earned from advertising and signage.

I know what you're thinking; the last thing you want to do is negotiate the lease of a tiny piece of real estate with a store owner, purchase an ATM, install it, insure it, and maintain it. I totally get it! I own dozens of ATMs all across the country by model and serial number, and I've never laid eyes, much less a hand, on any of them. I simply write a check, and these ATMs are purchased, installed, operated, and maintained by third parties. Every month since February of 2018, even through the duration of the COVID pandemic, I have received a check for $2,155. This cash flow continues for a total of seven years. At the end of seven years, the ATMs will be old, likely outdated, and will be sold.

So, what did I have to invest to receive this stream of cash? I purchased six ATMs for $104,000. The monthly cash flow coming back to me is $2,155 per month or $25,860 per year for a total of $181,020 over seven years.

In the internal rate of return (IRR) calculation below in the second block, the line items are simply the net cash in or net cash out—cash out represented by a negative number—over the seven years. In year one, I purchased the six machines for $104K and received $25,860 back, so my net cash flow for year one was -$78,140—$104K less $25,860. My net cash flow in years two through seven will be $25,860. The end result is an IRR of 23.98 percent.

| | |
|---|---|
| $104,000 | Initial Investment |
| $2,155 | Monthly Cash |
| $25,860 | Annual Total Cash |
| $181,020 | 7 Years Total Cash |

| Year | Cash Out/In | Explanation |
|---|---|---|
| 1 | -$78,140 | $104k less $25,860 |
| 2 | $25,860 | |
| 3 | $25,860 | |
| 4 | $25,860 | |
| 5 | $25,860 | |
| 6 | $25,860 | |
| 7 | $25,860 | |
| IRR | 23.98% | |

**Figure 3: ATM IRR Without Tax Savings**

But wait, there's more! The ATMs also came with a built-in tax advantage called depreciation. In this case, bonus depreciation. While bonus depreciation wasn't available when I purchased my first tranche of ATMs, it is available today under the current tax laws.

So, let's recalculate the IRR considering bonus depreciation. My initial investment was $104K. The monthly cash flow coming back to me is $2,155 per month or $25,860 per year for a total of $181,020 over seven years. Depreciation is the new element in this calculation. I received a deduction or expense of $104K in the same year I purchased the ATMs. I can use this to offset the ATM income itself or other passive income. For this example, I'll use it to offset the ATM income.

This means that I paid $0 income tax on the first $104K of ATM income. With an annual ATM income of $25,860, I will mostly deplete my $104K deduction in four years—$25,860 x 4 = $103,440. Let's look at the numbers.

My net cash out in the first year is now $71,934—$104K less $25,860 less $6,206 in tax savings. How did I come up with the $6,206? If I'm in a 24 percent tax bracket, 24 percent of $25,860 is $6,206. My net cash in years two through four will be $32,066—$25,860 plus $6,206. At the end of year four, I will have used almost all my $104K depreciation—$25,860 x 4 = $103,440.

In years five through seven, I'm back to my net cash flow of $25,860. The IRR in this scenario will be 35.20 percent, an 11.22 percent increase over the previous example.

Keep in mind that I'm not a CPA or a financial advisor, and this is an oversimplification of depreciation and how it's calculated. What I'm trying to illustrate is the advantage of investing in an asset that has a built-in tax advantage. In this case, an 11.22 percent increase in your return!

---

**Easy money!** My ATM investment delivered an additional 11.22 percent return on investment (ROI) simply because of the built-in tax advantage of bonus depreciation. I didn't take on extra risk to gain an additional 11.22 percent return. I simply picked an investment on the hierarchy instead of sitting in the shadows. Are you in the shadow of the pyramid and missing out on life-changing ROIs for you and your family?

| | |
|---|---|
| $104,000 | Initial Investment |
| $2,155 | Monthly Cash |
| $25,860 | Annual Total Cash |
| $181,020 | 7 Years Total Cash |
| $6,206 | Annual Tax Savings |

| Year | Cash Out/In | Explanation |
|---|---|---|
| 1 | -$71,934 | $104k less $25,860 |
| 2 | $32,066 | $25,860 plus $6,206 |
| 3 | $32,066 | $25,860 plus $6,206 |
| 4 | $32,066 | $25,860 plus $6,206 |
| 5 | $25,860 | |
| 6 | $25,860 | |
| 7 | $25,860 | |
| IRR | 35.20% | |

**Figure 4: ATM IRR With Tax Savings**

You might be wondering if the money I receive as the ATM owner is based on the ATM fees, then how is it that I receive exactly the same amount of money each month? Great question! After all, the number of transactions at each ATM varies day to day. I receive what's called a "blended return."

Instead of receiving a varying amount of money each month depending on the number of transactions of each ATM, my ATMs are managed as a group with hundreds of other ATMs. Regardless of each ATM's performance in the group, all participants receive the same $2,155 per month.

What I've described here is not a hypothetical example; I've invested in ATMs numerous times. With these ATMs, you get at least a 23.98 percent IRR, more depending on your tax situation.

Are ATM investments risky? That's a question that only each investor can answer. They have many of the same risks as any other investment: economic cycles, systemic risks, poor management, political and social unrest, war, natural disaster, technology risks, and so on. Investing in ATMs offers no liquidity; you're in it for the seven-year term. As far as withstanding the economic and systemic risk and the social and political unrest that 2020 threw at us, so far, at least, the ATMs have passed the test, delivering a durable and reliable stream of income throughout.

# CHAPTER 5

# Advantages and Disadvantages of Alternatives

As you move up the pyramid, you'll find many incredible advantages to these investments, one disadvantage, and two items that I consider neutral. Let's look at each one in detail.

- Greater Financial Education Required
- Diversification Increases
- Cash Flow Increases
- Returns Increase

- Insurability Increases
- The Ability to Use Leverage Increases
- Liquidity Decreases
- Volatility Decreases
- Risk - Neutral
- Tax Efficiency Increases
- Control Increases
- Asset Protection Increases
- Accredited Investors Only - Neutral

## Greater Financial Education Required

It requires greater financial education to invest in alternatives—at least if you want to succeed at it—and I consider this an advantage. Anytime we get smarter or learn something new, that's a good thing.

Some will say, "But Chris, that's work." Yes, it is. Work is usually a prerequisite to success and achievement. As Thomas A. Edison put it, "Opportunity is missed by most people because it is dressed in overalls and looks like work."

A good example where expanded financial education is required is investment real estate—whether it be a single-family rental, apartment building, or commercial space. If you want to invest in one of these, you'll likely need a bank loan. To obtain that loan, and depending on which type of building you're purchasing, you'll need to show your creditworthiness and the building's financial viability. For example, you'll need to show the banker things like net operating income, capitalization rate, and debt coverage ratio. If you don't know these terms, let alone speak to them intelligently, guess what? No bank loan and no building.

Looking back at the ATM example, you wouldn't just go out and purchase six ATMs without knowing anything about the business. Where would you place them, how much would you pay the store owner where they will be located, and what vendors are available to service and maintain them?

As I mentioned in Chapter 3, it requires almost *no* financial education to invest in conventional investments! In less than thirty minutes, you can go to any of the online trading platforms—Schwab, Fidelity, or TD Ameritrade, for example—and once you've funded the account, you can buy and sell stocks, bonds, mutual funds, and ETFs to your heart's desire. You might not even know what an ETF is!

But wait, it gets even better! If your company offers a 401K, it might even auto-enroll you in its 401K, selecting both the amount deducted from each paycheck and the mix of mutual funds in which you'll invest.

## Diversification Increases

As you move up the hierarchy, you gain *real* diversification, and diversification is an advantage. Diversification is one way to manage risk in a portfolio. By having different types of investments, you decrease the possibility that your entire portfolio will be affected by something that affects one type of investment, asset class, or a specific industry.

Most people don't realize that when they follow the conventional wisdom of having a *balanced portfolio* of stock, bonds, mutual funds, and ETFs, they have almost no diversification at all. They are diversified only within the paper asset class.

To fully explain this, I need to discuss how assets and investments are categorized, and I've created the two visual aids below to assist with the explanation. First, we've already discussed the two major categories, alternative and conventional investments. In the visual aids below, conventional investments are orange, and alternatives are green.

Beyond that, all investments fall into one of four smaller asset classes. According to CPA Tom Wheelwright, they are:

- Paper—stocks, bonds, mutual funds, ETFs, cash, notes, cash value life insurance

- Real Assets—real estate, business equipment
- Commodities—precious metals, oil, natural gas, grains, beef
- Businesses—private ownership
  - Cryptocurrency might actually be a class unto itself

Alternative investments include real assets, commodities, businesses, and also notes and cash value life insurance (from the paper assets class).

> **Important Point!** Do you see that in the world of investable assets, a well-diversified portfolio of stocks, bonds, mutual funds, and ETFs is all in the paper asset class—shown in orange? Your well-diversified portfolio isn't diversified at all. It contains no real assets, commodities, or businesses, all of which fall under the larger umbrella of alternative investments—shown in green. Like I mentioned before, you're in the shadow of the pyramid.

ATMs are real assets, business equipment.

| Paper | Real Assets | Commodities | Businesses |
|---|---|---|---|
| Stocks | Real Estate | Precious Metals | Private Shares |
| Bonds | Business Equipment | Oil | |
| Mutual Funds | | Natural Gas | |
| ETFs | | Grains | |
| Cash | | Beef | |
| Cash Value Life Insurance | | | |
| Notes | | | |

| |
|---|
| Conventional Investments |
| Alternative Investments |

**Figure 5: Asset Classes 1**

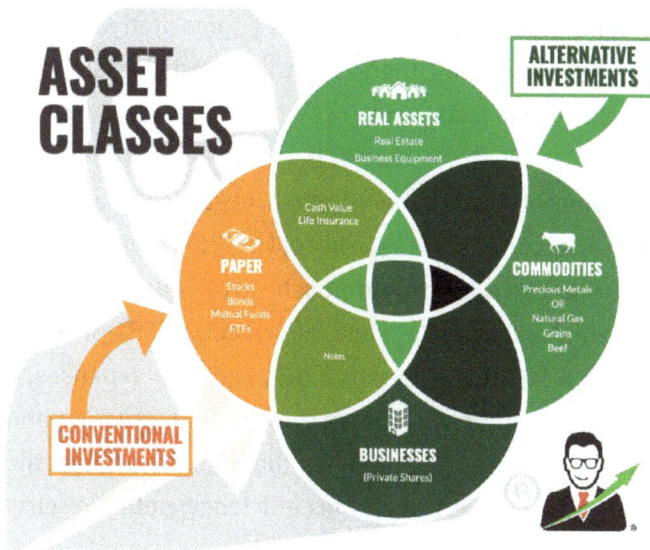

**Figure 6: Asset Classes 2**

## Cash Flow Increases

Increased cash flow—or any cash flow at all—is an advantage. As you move up the pyramid, many of the investments provide cash flow.

Cash flow isn't even a consideration for most conventional investors. They buy stocks, bonds, mutual funds, and ETFs hoping that these assets will appreciate over time. The way you turn these assets into cash is by selling them. Unless a conventional investor has a portfolio of dividend-producing stocks or is doing some pretty sophisti-cated options trading, there is very little cash flow amongst conventional investments.

When you get on the pyramid, notes, residential real estate, private lending, commercial real estate, and business equipment can all provide cash flow. One example is residential real estate, a single-family rental (SFR)—imagine you buy a $150K house, rent it out, and after expenses, it yields $750 per month. You get the monthly cash flow, and if the house appreciates, you get that too. You also get the advantages of leverage and tax efficiency, but I'll discuss that in another section.

Going back to my ATM example, the ATMs produce $2,155 per month in cash flow.

**Returns Increase**

The higher the ROI, the better. As you move up the pyramid, ROI increases.

So, what kind of returns can you expect from the stock market? As I mentioned in Chapter 3, the typical investor's average annual return is only 5.19 percent. After taking inflation and taxes into consideration, your returns are now in the low single digits.

If you're getting an annual ROI of less than 5 percent, you need a lot of money to retire, at least based on the conventional wisdom of amassing a huge portfolio of stocks, bonds, mutual funds, and ETFs and then selling off shares in retirement to fund your lifestyle. Most Americans don't invest a lot of money. When you multiply minimal investing by a small ROI, you get *disaster*—not enough money to retire or an impoverished retirement lifestyle.

As an alternative investor, I routinely get ROIs of 15 percent to 30 percent. Even if I subscribed to the conventional retirement wisdom, which I don't, I would need to invest much more money with returns below 5 percent than I do with returns in the 15 percent to 30 percent range.

When I tell people I routinely get 15 percent to 30 percent returns, their heads practically explode. They probably think I'm a liar, a crook, or both. It's because returns like this are just unheard of in the shadow of the pyramid. A conventional investor might occasionally see returns like these, but certainly not consistently.

What were the returns on my ATM investment? They were 23.98 percent without the tax advantages and 35.20 percent with the tax advantages. And this has been consistent since 2018 to the date of this writing, including during the COVID pandemic! *Life is better on the hierarchy.*

## Insurability Increases ⬆

As you move up the hierarchy, the ability to insure your investments increases. This is an advantage.

Insurance is a contract an individual or entity can purchase to protect one's assets against certain losses. You can also insure high-value items like your car, personal residence, boat, motorcycle, or airplane.

With conventional investments, you cannot go to an insurance agency and buy a policy to protect your stocks, bonds, and mutual funds from losses due to market conditions or systemic events.* You wouldn't dream of buying a house and not insuring it against destruction from fire, flood, or earthquake. Conventional investors, however, will spend their lifetimes working and pour hundreds of thousands of dollars into the stock market, then leave that money wide open to destruction resulting from a market crash, political event, war, pandemic, and so on.

Let's take an alternative investment like an apartment building. Not only can you insure the building, but if you purchased it with the help of a bank loan, the bank would *require* you to maintain a certain level of insurance as a condition of the loan.

Insurance companies are in the business of analyzing and protecting against risk. I think it says something about conventional investments' quality and stability that these assets are mostly uninsurable.

The ATMs I mentioned earlier are insured.

*\* I'm not an expert in this area, but it is possible to protect a stock portfolio against loss using options. It's a sophisticated kind of trading not widely used by the average investor.*

### The Ability to Use Leverage Increases

The ability to use leverage—obtain debt—to purchase assets is an advantage. As you move up the pyramid, your ability to use leverage increases.

In the financial world, leverage is another word for debt. If you remember back to your school days, there are six simple machines: lever, wheel and axle, pulley, inclined plane, wedge, and screw. What's the significance of these machines? These machines allow you to magnify your efforts.

Let's say there is a decorative, one hundred fifty-pound, round rock in your yard that is half above ground and half below ground. You need to move it fifteen feet from one side of your driveway to the other. If you were Dwayne Johnson

"The Rock," you'd just pick it up and carry it across the driveway. For us mere mortals, we'd roll it, but we might not even have enough strength to break the soil's friction and get it out of its hole to start rolling it. So, we'd dig around the rock until we can get a lever—the lever being a long piece of wood or steel—down near the bottom of the rock. The lever magnifies our strength and enables us to lift the rock out of its hole so we can roll it across the driveway.

Now back to the financial lever, debt. You're starting your investing career and want to start out with a bang, so you go to a bank and tell them you have a $20K down payment and would like to borrow $80K to purchase a $100K portfolio of mutual funds. After the banker gets done laughing, he'll politely tell you that they don't loan money to buy conventional investments.

Some conventional investors have and will continue to argue with me on this point because they consider buying stocks on margin as using leverage. With margin trading, you can buy stocks, bonds, and mutual funds with money borrowed from the brokerage firm. The brokerage firm will loan you a percentage of your portfolio's value to buy publicly traded securities. If you have a $100K portfolio, the brokerage firm might lend you $50K to purchase additional assets. To me, this is more like a home equity line of credit where you're able to borrow and use an asset you already own as collateral. You're not actually acquiring the assets with a loan.

With an alternative investment such as real estate, it's *uncommon* not to use leverage. Most investors don't have $150K cash to buy the SFR or $750K to buy the small apartment building. Just like when moving the rock across the driveway, alternative investors use leverage in the form of a loan to magnify the purchasing power of the money they do have.

Banks are in the business of lending—making money with other peoples' money. It says something about conventional investments' quality and stability when banks won't loan against these assets.

Not only does leverage increase your buying power, but it has a dramatic effect on ROI. Let's look at two examples:

### Joe Conventional

- On January 1, Joe purchases $100K worth of mutual funds with cash.
- On December 31 of the same year, his investment is worth $110K.
- What was Joe's ROI for the year? 10%.

- $10,000 increase in value divided by his $100,000 investment = 10% ROI.

### Susie Alternative

- On January 1, Susie purchases a $100K SFR with a $20K down payment and an $80K bank loan.
- On December 31 of the same year, her SFR is worth $110K.
- What was Susie's ROI for the year? 50%.
- $10,000 increase in value divided by her $20,000 investment = 50% ROI.

> **And people say debt is bad!** Do you see that the value of both investments increased by the same amount, $10,000? Why was Susie's ROI 50 percent and Joe's 10 percent? Because Susie only invested $20K. She borrowed the other $80K from the bank, but she gets the rewards of owning the entire building even though she only put up $20K of the money to buy it. This example illustrates how leverage magnifies your returns. Caution! Leverage also magnifies the downside as well, so you have to use debt carefully.

What about my ATMs? I obtained private loans to buy some of my tranches of ATMs but not a bank loan. I do know an investor who was able to get a bank loan to purchase ATMs, however.

Finally, many successful and popular gurus tell you to get out of debt—that debt is bad. They would be right when it comes to consumer debt; that is a bad kind of debt. The correct type of debt coupled with the right type of cash-flowing asset is good debt, and it will make you rich.

> **Keep in mind!** When you do it correctly, you don't make the loan payments; the asset does. The tenants in the SFR or apartment building and the ATM users ultimately make the loan payments.

## Liquidity Decreases

Having liquidity is an advantage. As you move up the hierarchy, liquidity mostly decreases, so this is a disadvantage for alternative investments. In fact, it is the only disadvantage alternatives have compared to conventional investments.

Investopedia defines liquidity as the ease with which an asset or security can be converted into ready cash without affecting its market price. Conventional investments are very liquid; they can be quickly sold and converted into cash.

As you move up the pyramid and acquire alternative investments, they are generally less liquid and harder to convert to cash. You can't push a button on a computer and sell your residential or commercial real estate. Some exceptions include precious metals and cryptocurrency.

My ATMs are illiquid. I'm pretty much in that deal for the seven-year term.

## Volatility Decreases

Unless you're a day trader and profit from market volatility, volatility is negative. As you move up the pyramid, volatility largely decreases, and this is an advantage. Some exceptions are precious metals and cryptocurrency.

Volatility has to do with how quickly and how widely an asset's price fluctuates.

On the hierarchy, real estate prices tend to change slowly. While some U.S. markets are overheated, an SFR's value doesn't typically go from $100K on Tuesday to $150K on Wednesday. Its value changes more slowly over time. This is because it is illiquid; it's hard to convert the house to cash. If you could sell SFRs with the push of a button, they would be volatile, just like stocks.

However, a stock, mutual fund, or ETF can sell for $100 per share on Tuesday at 3:00 pm and sell for $150 per share on Tuesday at 3:15 pm—an extremely volatile 50 percent increase. Most wouldn't complain about the 50 percent increase in value in fifteen minutes; it's the 50 percent decrease that is unsettling. Except for cash and CDs, most conventional assets are highly volatile.

There is an inverse relationship between liquidity and volatility. Liquid assets are volatile, and illiquid assets are non-volatile.

> **Key point!**
> Liquid Assets = Volatile (stocks, bonds, mutual funds)
> Illiquid Assets = Non-Volatile (SFRs, apartments)

My ATMs are illiquid; they can't be sold at the push of a button and are therefore non-volatile.

I can't leave this section without touching on the stock market's volatility due to emotional trading. When I invest, I look at fundamental things like the management team, cash flow, ROI, tax advantages, and how likely an investment is to withstand an economic or business downturn. Nowhere in my analysis do I factor in emotions. However, emotional responses are a regular occurrence in the stock market. The prices of assets go up and down wildly due to emotions, what people feel about things like:

- A banker making statements about the direction of interest rates
- A third-world dictator launching an ICBM test
- A natural disaster occurring in another part of the world
- A politician tweeting something stupid or offensive

None of the above likely has an immediate effect on the business fundamentals of companies like Apple, Boeing, or Campbells Soup. Still, conventional investors can and do see their portfolios' values swing wildly due to emotional trading based on the above points as well as high-frequency computerized trading. For the most part, I choose not to participate in this volatile marketplace that is largely based on emotions and computerized trading and disconnected from business and economic fundamentals and reality!

At TheProlificInvestor.net, I wrote an article about this. See *Blog #5 – What's Wrong with the Stock Market Anyway?*

**Risk - Neutral**

Except for U.S. Treasury securities, which are generally considered risk-free, there is some risk with every investment.

For this reason, I consider risk on the Hierarchy of Investors to be neutral; risk exists with both conventional and alternative investments.

Some investments on the pyramid and in the shadow are simply risky by their nature—drilling for oil and junk bonds, for example. Drilling for oil is an alternative investment, and junk bonds are a conventional investment. A publicly traded company in a new industry is risky, as is a privately held company in a new industry. The publicly traded company is a conventional investment, and the privately held company is an alternative.

The big difference is that conventional investments are heavily regulated by the Securities and Exchange Commission (SEC). While laws pertain to alternative investments, oversight is so minimal that they are generally considered unregulated.

This sets up a situation where conventional investors think their investments are safe and alternatives are inherently risky or even scams. Having talked with many conventional investors about alternatives, they ask me questions about my investments they would never ask about their own— clearly a double standard.

- Is your investment guaranteed?
- Is your investment a Ponzi scheme?
- What prevents the organizer from running off with the money?

Firstly, my investments aren't guaranteed, and neither are theirs unless they invest in U.S. Treasury securities. Secondly, fraud, evil people, and incompetence exist everywhere on the hierarchy. I will concede, however, that outright fraud is probably harder to commit with conventional investments than it is with alternatives.

This is why greater financial education is required with alternatives—the SEC hasn't done the due diligence for you. However, the cost of the SEC's due diligence comes in the form of lower returns to you, the investor. All that compliance with SEC rules and regulations is an expense to the business and is money that *does not* end up in your pocket. So, *get off your A$$*, do your due diligence, and keep more money for you and your family!

When researching an alternative investment, you have one huge advantage—you can talk with the principals on the phone or meet them for lunch. You can't call up the CEO of Apple, Boeing, or Campbell Soup before buying their stock. One of my favorite ways to get a feel for the principal or syndicator's character is to take her to breakfast and see how she treats the wait staff, people who can do nothing for her and will likely not invest in her business.

If you think your conventional investments are safe, if you believe that fraud and unethical behavior don't exist, think again.

- Wells Fargo—Opened fake accounts under customers' names
- Volkswagen—Put special software in its cars to hide unlawful emissions levels
- Enron—Cooked its books to make the company look more profitable than it was
- WorldCom—Cooked its books
- Waste Management—Cooked its books
- Tyco International—Executives stole from the company and cooked the books
- HealthSouth—Cooked its books

As far as my ATM investment goes, I called the syndicator on the phone before I ever invested, and I've had numerous conversations with him on the phone and in-person since my initial investment. Additionally, my ATMs have delivered stable and consistent monthly cash flow since February 2018 despite COVID and its aftermath.

## Tax Efficiency Increases ⬆

Tax efficiency increases as you move up the pyramid; in other words, you pay fewer taxes. This is an advantage.

As you move up the hierarchy, you have greater control over your tax burden, and you can pay less or even no taxes. See Blog #29 at TheProlificInvestor.net titled *President Trump Paid $750 In Taxes; I Paid $0*! You'll also find some of my other favorite tax stories at Blogs #28, #20, and #6.

It's always dangerous for a non-CPA-type person like me to write about taxes because I'm not an expert, and I'll probably get something wrong. In fact, I've read *very little* of the actual tax code. On the other hand, I've been quite successful at lowering and, in some cases eliminating taxes altogether. Thus my story is actually a testament to the fact that you *don't* need to be a tax expert or a CPA to reduce or eliminate taxes.

I've successfully reduced my taxes by listening to smart people like Tom Wheelwright through his Wealthability Podcast and book *Tax-Free Wealth: How to Build Massive Wealth by Permanently Lowering Your Taxes*. Additionally, I belong to several investor mastermind groups where we regularly discuss the changing tax landscape and how we'll respond to those changes to legally and ethically pay fewer taxes. Finally, I have a good CPA with whom I can validate my ideas and get assistance implementing my strategies.

Entire books have been written on taxes, which I'm not qualified to do. To provide value and keep within my lane when it comes to my knowledge on this topic, I'm going to focus on the two things that have helped me reduce and, in some cases, eliminate taxes:

- Choosing the right type of income
- Choosing who earns the income

However, before I can address these two topics, I need to review the difference between how individuals and businesses are taxed. Buckle up!

### How Businesses Are Taxed

Let's think about how businesses are taxed. *Businesses pay taxes on their net income.* Businesses receive their revenue, then deduct all their operating expenses-wages, utilities, interest, cost of goods sold, rent, insurance, supplies, memberships, meals, travel, advertising, legal, and so forth. Only after deducting all their expenses do businesses pay tax on what's leftover—their net income.

## How Individuals Are Taxed

Now, let's think about how individuals are taxed. *Individuals pay taxes on their gross income.* You receive your paycheck, and then the government takes its share of taxes from your gross income. Later, you get to reconcile by taking the few allowable deductions on your tax return that are available to individuals and couples. Even though you have many of the same expenses as a business-utilities, interest, rent, insurance, supplies, memberships, meals, travel, and legal, you don't get to deduct these expenses.

It might not be fair, but it's the way it is. The government is telling you that it values businesses. It believes they bring value to the economy by creating jobs and providing goods and services that people need or want. In exchange, the government gives businesses more favorable tax treatment than it does to individuals.

So, stop fighting the government and complaining about your taxes. Why not make them your partner and start a business so you too can get more favorable tax treatment? You're not a business person or an entrepreneur, you say. Well, you're an investor, or at least you want to be, or you wouldn't be reading this book.

Why not switch your investment income from being received by you to being received by a business by making your investments in the name of a business instead of your name? Now the income from your investments gets the same favorable tax treatment as businesses, think Apple, Boeing, and Campbell Soup.

## The Types of Income

There are five types of income: earned income, ordinary income, investment income, gifts/inheritance income, and passive income. I'm omitting gifts/inheritance from this discussion.

- Earned Income – wages, salaries, self-employment
- Ordinary Income – pension, 401K, IRA
- Investment Income – capital gains, interest, dividends
- Passive Income – real asset and business income (you don't personally manage)

If you're an employee and receive a W-2, this is earned income. This type of income is taxed at the highest level, and you have the fewest deductions, which may include mortgage interest, 401K and IRA contributions, charitable giving, and so on.

If you're retired and receive a pension or take distributions from a 401K or IRA, this is ordinary income. You're still taxed at a high level and have few deductions, but you don't pay social security and Medicare taxes on this income.

If you're a conventional investor, the income you receive from your stock, bond, ETF, and mutual fund portfolio is investment income. There are lower tax rates on some of this income but still few deductions.

If you're an alternative investor and have ownership in real assets, like real estate, or businesses that you don't directly manage, this is *passive income, the mack daddy of all income types.* This income can be taxed the least or not at all due to depreciation and numerous deductions, which can be taken when received by a business structure. Stay tuned.

For visual learners like me, I've represented the types of income in Figure 7. As you move from the top to the bottom of the figure—from earned income to passive income—two things happen, taxes get lower, and deductions increase. To put it another way, you go from the bad type of income to the good type of income.

| High Tax | Earned Income | Wages salaries, self-employment | Few Deductions |
| | Ordinary Income | Pension, 401K, IRA | |
| | Investment Income | Capital gains, interest, dividends | |
| Low Tax | Passive Income | Real estate and businesses (you don't personally manage) | More Deductions |

Bad
Better
Best

**Figure 7: Types of Income**

Let's revisit our old friends Joe Conventional and Susie Alternative to see what types of income they earn and who earns it. This time, however, I'll add The Prolific Investor to the mix and see what he does.

## Joe Conventional

Joe Conventional has a job, so most of his income is earned income, the bad kind. Joe invests in stocks and mutual funds, so he also has investment income, better than earned income but still not the best. All of Joe's income is earned by Joe, where he gets taxed the worst way, on his gross income. Joe is very much like most Americans and is getting hammered by taxes. You might even be like Joe. Don't worry; you *can* do something about this.

## Joe Conventional

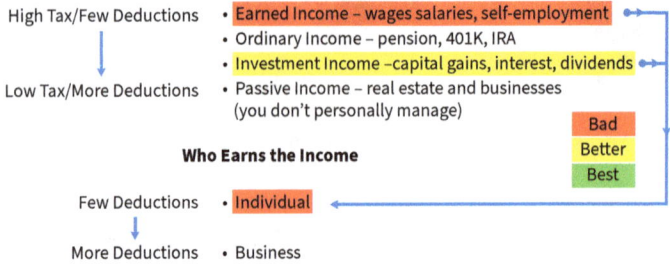

**Figure 8: Joe Conventional Income Example**

## Susie Alternative

Like Joe, Susie has a job, so most of her income is also the bad kind, earned income. Also, like Joe, Susie invests in stocks and mutual funds, which is a better type of income but still not the best. Here's where Susie departs from Joe. While Susie's earned income is earned by Susie, she set up a company, Susie Alternative, LLC, and Susie's investment income flows through this business and is taxed on the net income of her business, just like Apple, Boeing, and Campbell Soup.

## Susie Alternative

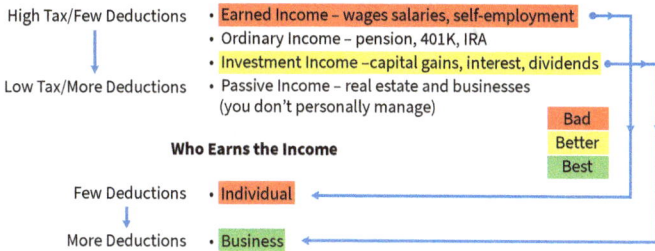

| | |
|---|---|
| High Tax/Few Deductions | • Earned Income – wages salaries, self-employment |
| | • Ordinary Income – pension, 401K, IRA |
| | • Investment Income –capital gains, interest, dividends |
| Low Tax/More Deductions | • Passive Income – real estate and businesses (you don't personally manage) |

Bad
Better
Best

**Who Earns the Income**

| | |
|---|---|
| Few Deductions | • Individual |
| More Deductions | • Business |

## Figure 9: Susie Alternative Income Example

### The Prolific Investor

Finally, let's look at how The Prolific Investor does things. First and most importantly, I *avoid* earned income like the plague. I don't engage in activities or investments that generate earned income. I seek out investments that generate passive income and come with that magical tax buster called *depreciation*. For me, this is primarily real estate.

Additionally, I don't make investments; my company, Chris Odegard, LLC, for this example, does all my investing. To sum it all up, I choose the best type of income to earn and choose to have that income earned by a business. Ok, I exaggerated a little bit for the sake of this example. I do earn some ordinary income because of the time I previously spent in the dark, in the shadow of the hierarchy, before I knew better. But I purposely don't acquire new sources of ordinary income because it's hard to shelter.

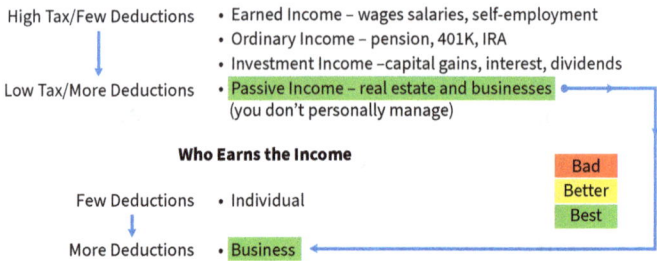

**Figure 10: The Prolific Investor Income Example**

Figure 11 brings this all together, showing the types of income Joe, Susie, and The Prolific Investor earn and who earns it.

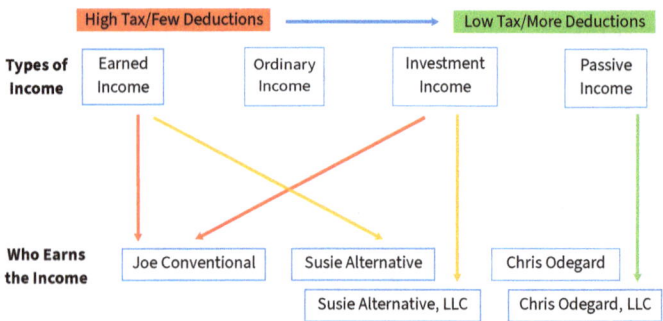

**Figure 11: Joe, Susie, and The Prolific Investor Income Comparison**

When you're an employee like Susie and Joe, you just don't have many options to reduce your taxes, except the route Susie took, which was to have some of her income flow through a business.

An option Susie, Joe, or any employee might try is asking your employer if you can switch to an independent contractor role. Now, your former employer pays the company you set up specifically for this purpose, and your former W-2 income would now be revenue to your business. You'd receive all the great tax benefits that businesses receive. Obviously, you need to figure out whether this is even an option with your employer and do the cost-benefit analysis of both options.

You'll note that I omitted 401Ks and IRAs in my examples as a way for Susie and Joe to reduce their earned income. This is certainly an option and one that most American's use. I'm going to make a *bold* statement that many of you might not like.

**If I knew in my twenties what I know today, I would *never* have put a dime in a pre-tax IRA or 401K!**

### What's Wrong with 401Ks and IRAs

I know this statement probably goes against every fiber in your body, but 401Ks and IRAs, specifically those where you are limited to investing in stocks, bonds, mutual funds, and ETFs, are *terrible* investment vehicles. This topic deserves an entire book, and whole books have been written about it. To learn more, read *401(k)aos: How Our Dream of Retirement Became a Nightmare of Chaos* by Andy Tanner.

In my twenties, when I started my first full-time job, I encountered the 401K for the first time. I asked a person I knew, liked, and trusted what he thought about the 401K. He said I should put as much money in the 401K as my employer would allow. He was a conventional investor, and I don't blame him for that advice as it was all he knew. However, as I mentioned in the introduction, following that advice cost me *millions* of dollars over the following decades.

Let me briefly tell you what's wrong with the typical pre-tax 401K and IRA.

### They Assume You'll Be Less Successful In The Future

When you put money into these vehicles, you postpone paying the taxes on that money until the future…when you'll be in a lower tax bracket. At least that's what the so-call experts tell you. We should all be extremely *insulted*. What they're really saying to you is that, after a lifetime of working, earning, and investing, you'll be less successful—make less money—in the future than you do today.

I've coined a saying I often use, "I try not to get old and stupid at the same time." After a lifetime of working, earning, and investing, being less successful and earning less money in the future sounds stupid and like a failed plan to me—or the lack of plan altogether.

If we did things right, we should be at the top of our game, at the pinnacle of success when we choose to stop working, and that could actually mean a higher tax bracket in retirement than in our working years.

### They Assume Tax Brackets Will Be The Same In The Future

Let's say the experts are wrong, and you're not less successful in the future than you are today, but you're equally successful. You have the same income in retirement that you had when you were working. Do you really think that tax brackets will be the same in the future? Has our government, or any government for that matter, ever needed or wanted less tax revenue?

Let's assume Joe Conventional has earned income today of $100K per year. That puts Joe in a 24 percent tax bracket, and he will owe $24K in taxes.

Thirty years have passed, and Joe is now retired and feels very proud that he still has $100K per year of income, even in retirement. Due to the government's insatiable appetite for borrowing, printing, and spending, Joe's $100K is now taxed at 30 percent instead of 24 percent. Now Joe owes $30K in taxes instead of $24K. Joe would have been better off skipping the 401K and IRA altogether.

| | Income | Tax Bracket | Tax Obligation |
|---|---|---|---|
| Working | $100,000 | 24% | $24,000 |
| Retirement | $100,000 | 30% | $30,000 |

**Figure 12: Working Versus Retirement Tax Brackets and Tax Obligation**

## They Convert Investment Income To Ordinary Income

One of the reasons businesses and investors get better tax treatment than individuals is that they are taking a risk. Starting businesses and investing in those businesses involves risk, the potential loss of capital. The government rewards those who take those risks through better tax treatment.

Let's go back to Joe again, earning $100K per year in retirement. Joe's $100K per year comes from distributions from his 401K and is taxed as ordinary income at 24 percent ($24K), as discussed in the example above.

What if Joe had never put a dime in a 401K and instead, he bought the same stocks and mutual funds with after-tax money through Charles Schwab? Now in retirement, Joe would be taking distributions from his Charles Schwab account, and his $100K per year would be taxed, not as ordinary income, but as investment income at long-term capital gains rates, currently at 15 percent. So instead of paying $24K per year in taxes, Joe would pay $15K per year.

The 401K has converted what would have been investment income (a better kind of income) to ordinary income (the worst type of income). So far, I'm failing to see the benefits of this 401K investment vehicle.

| Income Source | Income | Tax Bracket | Tax Obligation |
|---|---|---|---|
| 401k | $100,000 | 24% | $24,000 |
| Schwab Brokerage | $100,000 | 15% | $15,000 |

## Figure 13: Income Source Tax Bracket and Tax Obligation

### They Limit The Assets You Can Buy

We already learned that assets fall into two large groups, conventional investments, and alternative investments. Beyond that, they are classified into paper assets, real assets, commodities, and businesses. For a review of asset classes, see Figures 5 and 6.

The typical 401K and IRA only allow you to purchase and hold *some*, not all, paper assets—stocks, bonds, mutual funds, and ETFs. Why is this? No law or regulation is preventing the plans from allowing you to purchase SFRs, notes, apartment buildings, ATMs, or oil wells from your IRA or 401K.

In fact, the only things the IRS says you cannot invest in with your 401K and IRA are life insurance, types of derivatives, antiques and collectibles, real estate for personal use, alcohol, and most but not all coins.

It's the plan administrator themselves, Fidelity, Vanguard, T. Rowe Price, for example, that limit you to *some* paper assets. Why? Paper assets provide an easy and automated source of revenue for them, just as they do for financial planners, as discussed in Chapter 3.

Most people don't know that *you can* set up a self-directed IRA or 401K, where you are the administrator and can invest in anything you want except the aforementioned items prohibited by the IRS. I recommend the self-directed 401K over the self-directed IRA. Simply go to your favorite search engine and type in "self-directed 401k" to find a company that can set this up for you.

I have invested in apartment buildings, businesses, and cryptocurrency with self-directed 401K and IRA money.

### They Have Numerous Other Restrictions

Beyond limiting the assets in which you can invest, 401Ks and IRAs have restrictions related to annual contributions, when you can withdraw money, and even requirements to withdraw money at a certain age. Isn't this your money for your benefit? It sure seems like these vehicles are mostly designed to benefit someone else.

## Control Increases

Control increases as you move up the hierarchy. This is an advantage.

Control is a good thing; we all want it. With conventional investments, you have no control over your investment's performance. When you buy a stock, bond, or mutual fund, the control of that investment's performance is entirely in the hands of other people. You can't do anything to improve the performance of Apple, Boeing, or Campbell Soup. All you can do is buy, hold, or sell.

If you're on the pyramid and you own real estate, you have lots of control. You can raise or lower the rent, change marketing strategies, offer incentives, add amenities like an ensuite washer and dryer, remodel the interior, and increase curb appeal with paint and landscaping.

Looking back at my ATM example again, if certain ATMs aren't seeing enough transactions, the management company can move them to a better location with more foot traffic to increase transactions.

## Asset Protection Increases

Asset protection increases as you move up the hierarchy. This is an advantage.

Most alternative investments don't automatically provide you with asset protection—cash value life insurance, syndication/limited partnerships are exceptions. They provide some asset protection by their very nature.

As you move up the pyramid, you gain more financial education and wealth. With that wealth comes an increasing desire to preserve and protect the wealth you've worked so hard to acquire.

"How can I lose my wealth?" you ask. We live in a litigious society, and anyone can sue you for any reason, regardless of whether their case has merit. "But I have insurance," you say, and you should. Nearly all the wealthy people I know follow a particular philosophy—when it comes to your wealth, you need both insurance and asset protection in the form of a business structure or trust. I'll discuss both later. This dual approach is sometimes referred to as "belt and suspenders."

Let's say Joe Conventional gets in an accident with his motor home, and someone is seriously injured. Joe is deemed to be partially at fault, and the injured party wants to sue. When an attorney is deciding whether it's worth his time to bring a case against Joe, he does an asset search to see what Joe owns. The attorney needs to know that he'll get paid via Joe's insurance or the assets he can seize if he takes on the case and wins.

In his research, the attorney finds that Joe owns everything in his name, his rental properties, boat, brokerage account, and classic car collection. The lawyer proceeds with the case and wins damages exceeding the amount of Joe's insurance, but not to worry, the attorney can get Joe's boat, rental properties, brokerage account, and classic car collection. Joe was an easy target and is wiped out!

Now let's look at Susie Alternative. Susie finds herself in the same position, partially at fault in a motor vehicle accident and the possible target of a lawsuit. A lawyer does an asset search on Susie and finds that Susie's house is in her name but has a first and second mortgage totaling 90 percent of the house's value. Beyond that, Susie appears to own nothing. Ergo, the lawyer declines to take the case against Susie as her insurance policy is not enough to adequately compensate him for his time and effort if he wins.

What wasn't readily apparent is that Susie has a sizable real estate portfolio owned through various companies and trusts. Susie was not an easy target, was not sued, and retained all her assets.

I don't know if there is such a thing as perfect asset protection—insurance, business structures, and trusts certainly help—but the bottom line is, don't be an easy target! You worked hard to get where you are. Isn't it worth your time, effort, and money to preserve what you've worked so hard to acquire?

## Accredited Investors Only - Neutral

I've put this as neutral because it depends on your current status. If you're already an accredited investor, this is irrelevant to you. If you're not accredited, this is a negative.

As you move up the hierarchy, you will find that *some investments* are only open to accredited investors. If you're not an accredited investor yet, you should strive to become one so you're not forever locked out of these investments. Not to worry, however, plenty of alternative investments are available to you.

As defined by the Securities and Exchange Commission (SEC), an accredited investor is a person with an annual income exceeding $200,000—$300,000 for joint income—for the last two years or a net worth exceeding $1 million excluding their primary residence.

Many alternative investments are not regulated by the SEC—all publicly traded stocks, bonds, mutual funds, and ETFs are highly regulated by the SEC. One of the SEC's tasks is to protect investors from unscrupulous deal organizers. Since alternative investments are unregulated, the way the SEC protects investors is by limiting these investments to high-income or high-net-worth people who won't be wiped out if they get into business with fraudulent people.

The last thing the SEC wants to happen is for grandma to lose her $100K life savings to an unethical deal organizer or a risky, unregulated investment and be dependent on the taxpayers for the rest of her life.

# CHAPTER 6

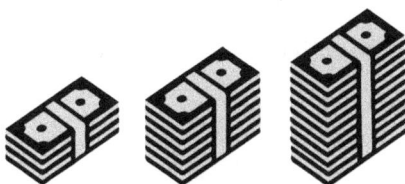

# Types of Ownership

As mentioned previously, asset protection is primarily gained through how you own assets—typically through a business or trust. In Chapter 5's Asset Protection Increases section, I gave some examples of how owning assets in a business versus personally can protect those assets in a lawsuit. This section will discuss some of the typical forms of ownership investors go through as they gain financial education and move up the pyramid.

## Personal Name

In the beginning, owning things in your name is all you know. As you begin to accumulate assets and liabilities—car, boat, motorcycle, personal residence, brokerage account, and so forth—you own these personally, and you have no asset protection with this form of ownership.

## 401Ks and IRAs

At some point, you're introduced to the retirement savings vehicles of IRAs and 401Ks, and these are attractive because of their simplicity, the deferral of taxes, and the employer match in some cases. With these vehicles, some of your paper assets are now owned by your IRA or 401K. Most people aren't even thinking about asset protection at this point, but IRAs and 401Ks do come with some asset protection, 401Ks more so than IRAs.

## Living Trusts

Joe Conventional eventually gets married, and he and his wife have two children. Joe starts to think about what will happen to his young family if he or his spouse dies prematurely. To that end, Joe and his wife purchase life insurance, and each get a will to ensure their assets are used to provide for the children if one or both of them is no longer in the picture.

What they didn't know is that a will is not enough to ensure the smooth transition of their asset ownership if one or both of them die. With only a will, an attorney is required to take their wills through probate, a legal process ensuring that the wills' instructions are carried out correctly. Probate complexity varies by state, but it can take thousands of dollars in legal fees and months to complete. All the while, the family is dealing with the death of one or more parents and may need money from the estate that is now tied up in a lengthy and expensive legal process.

Finally, Joe obtained better legal counsel, who advised him to set up a living trust in addition to the wills. The living trust allows Joe and his wife to bypass probate and instead have a successor trustee whom they appoint distribute or liquidate their assets per their instructions. The living trust provides no asset protection; it merely makes it less complicated and costly for your heirs to take over and use your estate assets as directed.

> **Important point!** It's not enough to just establish a living trust. You have to change the ownership of your assets and belongings from your name to the name of the trust. Joe's residence, cars, bank accounts, brokerage accounts, and any other valuable items need to be retitled in the name of the Joe Family Living Trust so that the trustee can manage these items.

## Business Structures

A typical initial step when venturing beyond conventional investments and moving up the hierarchy is obtaining an SFR. Many times, it even happens by accident. Someone decides to move up from a starter home to a bigger one, and somehow, they get the idea of just keeping the starter home and renting it out. Boom! In one fell swoop, they're an alternative investor in the real assets class. The great thing is that with one SFR, you can gain many of the benefits of alternative investments with one single investment—cash flow, diversification, leverage, insurability, returns, and control.

There is a tradeoff, however. Renting to the public exposes you and your personal assets to liability; unless you have a business structure, you're left unprotected, beyond the value of insurance policies. This is one example of where investors typically set up their first LLC and perhaps a management company. These entities provide the asset protection we talked about in the Asset Protection section with Suzie Alternative.

---

**Don't be fooled!** Just because you set up an LLC or Corporation doesn't mean you're immune from liability. If you commit fraud, a court can hold you personally liable. If you don't adhere to standard corporate formalities, a court can hold you personally responsible. Corporate formalities include things like:

- Holding annual and special meetings
- Maintaining meeting minutes
- Having separate business bank accounts
- Not commingling personal and business money

The term for when a court reaches inside the business and holds the owners personally liable is "piercing the corporate veil."

---

## Syndication/Limited Partnerships

A syndication and a limited partnership are technically two separate things, but I tend to comingle the terms when I describe the typical type of investing I do.

A syndication is when people, companies, or both pool their resources to consummate a business transaction that is too large for any of them to do individually. In a simple, relatable example, Suzie Alternative wants to buy a fifteen-unit apartment building for $1M, but she can't come up with the $300K down payment independently.

Suzie contacts her two best girlfriends, and they all agree to contribute $100K each towards the down payment and purchase the building together. Suzie has just created a syndication by pooling three people's resources to buy an asset she couldn't otherwise do alone.

The business arrangement between the three women could be a general partnership, a limited partnership, or something else. In this situation, Suzie decided to create a limited partnership. Suzie is a sophisticated real estate investor and brings her vast experience to the table in addition to her $100,000. Her girlfriends merely contribute the money— they have busy day jobs and want nothing to do with the apartment building's day-to-day operations. In this limited-partnership structure, Suzie, as the general partner, has all the decision-making power. The other two women are limited partners.

So, how does this ownership structure affect asset protection? The three women now own an apartment building and have rental agreements with fifteen tenants. This exposes them to liability. In a limited partnership, the general partner, Suzie, has unlimited liability. However, her two girlfriends, who are limited partners, have their liability capped at $100K, the value of their initial investment.

Most of the investments I do these days are syndications/limited partnerships, whereby my liability is limited to my initial investment. Some examples are apartment buildings, self-storage facilities, and coal-processing units.

My ATMs are not limited partnerships, but my ownership is via an LLC and not my name, thus providing me asset protection.

**Asset Protection Trusts**

I mentioned living trusts earlier, which have no asset protection but allow your heirs to manage and settle your affairs more efficiently when you pass. I also mentioned business structures, which provide asset protection, but their protections can be pierced for various reasons.

Investors who have climbed high on the hierarchy with a net worth of millions of dollars start looking for the most robust asset protection available, which is some type of asset protection trust (APT). Going into APTs in depth is beyond the scope of this book. If your net worth is in the millions, you probably already know about APTs. If not, now you do. Find an expert to see what is suitable for your specific situation.

CHAPTER 7

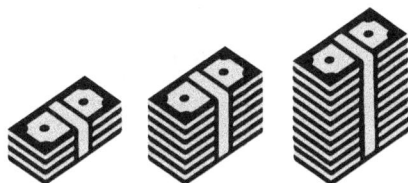

# Call to Action

In conclusion, two paths are available in the investing world. One choice is the well-traveled path of conventional investments—essentially mediocrity, where most people invest. The other option is the less-traveled path of alternative investments where the real money is made and where the wealthy invest. You don't have to be rich to invest in alternatives, but you do need financial education.

If you're like most people, you've been stuck in conventional investments all your life. Now that you've been shown the light, what are you going to do? You can act on your newfound knowledge or ignore it.

Someone once said, "Knowledge is power." That's a lie! Robert Helms and Russell Gray, The Real Estate Guys, have the following motto, "Education for Effective Action." In other words, knowledge is *not* power. Power comes from connecting knowledge with action, doing something with it! What are you going to do?

In case I haven't convinced you yet, let me show you the scorecard of alternatives versus conventional investments. In the graphic below are the thirteen categories I chose for comparing these two types of investments.

Of the thirteen categories, ten are advantages in favor of alternatives, one is an advantage for the conventional investments, and two are neutral. The only advantage of conventional investments is liquidity, but with liquidity comes its alter ego, volatility, so I often question whether liquidity is an advantage at all.

| | Alternative Investments | Conventional Investments |
|---|---|---|
| Accredited Investors Only | Neutral | Neutral |
| Asset Protection | Advantage | |
| Control | Advantage | |
| Tax Efficiency | Advantage | |
| Risk | Neutral | Neutral |
| Volatility | Advantage | |
| Liquidity | | Advantage |
| Leverage | Advantage | |
| Insurability | Advantage | |
| Return on Investment | Advantage | |
| Cash Flow | Advantage | |
| Diversification | Advantage | |
| Financial Education | Advantage | |

**Figure 14: Alternative Investments Versus Conventional Investments Scorecard**

With so many advantages, why wouldn't more people invest in alternatives? To reiterate what I mentioned before, it's easy, it's all we know, and there's money in it for other people, which drives all the advertising that bombards us daily. There is advertising for alternatives, but you won't find it on CNN, MSNBC, or Fox; you've got to seek some of your financial news from alternative sources. Do you see a pattern here?

Go to the Resources Page of my website at The ProlificIn-vestor.net and check out the books, podcasts, and other resources listed there. Here you will find people advertising and talking about alternatives.

Whether you've had a financial setback or perhaps are just not where you'd like to be financially, you owe it to yourself and your family to learn about alternative investments.

Some people think alternative investments should comprise a small percentage of your portfolio. I'm slightly different, as I invest almost exclusively in alternative investments. I drink my own Kool-Aid! I look at the chart above and ask myself, "Why would anyone invest primarily in conventional investments when it's overwhelmingly clear that they are so inferior to alternative investments?"

I know change is scary and hard for many people, but it's genuinely the only thing you can count on—things will be different tomorrow than they are today!

At this point, you've almost read this entire book. Hopefully you're convinced you that you need to start investing in alternatives and maybe even liquidate some of your conventional investments and turn them into alternatives. How do you get started?

## Know Your Numbers—Balance Sheet and Income Statement

You need to know your numbers, your net worth, and your net income. This means having and maintaining two financial statements, a balance sheet and an income statement. Having these will help you in the subsequent section on accredited investors.

A balance sheet includes your assets and liabilities; the number resulting when subtracting your liabilities from your assets is your net worth. When someone is a millionaire, their net worth, the bottom number on their balance sheet, is equal to or greater than $1M.

Things that go on your balance sheet as assets include:

- Cash
- Bank Accounts
- Life Insurance
- Brokerage Accounts
- Investment Real Estate
- Retirement Accounts

- Personal Residence—except when determining accredited investor status
- Vehicles
- Precious Metals

Things that go on your balance sheet as liabilities include:

- Mortgages
- Student Loans
- Vehicle Loans
- Credit Card Debt
- Other Liabilities

Your net worth is one measure of your success as an investor. The other is cash flow, which we'll discuss next with the income statement. Update your balance sheet at least once a year so that you can track your progress in building your wealth.

An income statement includes your income and expenses; the resulting number when subtracting your expenses from your income is your net income.

Things that go on your income statement as income include:

- Monthly Wages
- Rental Income

- Investment Income
- Other Income Sources

Things that go on your income statement as expenses include:

- Mortgages or Rent
- HELOC
- Vehicle Loans
- Credit Card
- Student Loans
- Utilities
- Insurance
- Groceries
- Other Expenses

Your net income or positive cash flow is the other measure of your success as an investor, but neither measure alone tells the whole story. You have to look at both numbers.

For example, if you own $2M worth of investment real estate that only breaks even, produces no positive cash flow, you're a *multimillionaire*, but you'll need a job because you have no cash flow to pay your bills. On the other hand, if your $2M worth of real estate generates $100K per year of positive cash flow, you don't need a job.

At the end of the day, you can't live off a large balance sheet unless it produces cash flow, or you can sell off portions of it periodically to produce the cash flow you need to live on; this is the traditional retirement philosophy.

The problem with building up a $2M portfolio of stocks, bonds, mutual funds, and ETFs and then periodically selling them off is that you might be forced to sell them at a time when the market is down. In this situation, you'll need to sell more shares to produce the same amount of cash flow and run the risk of running out of balance sheet to sell before you run out of life.

### Are You an Accredited Investor?

Now that you've got a balance sheet and an income statement, you can determine whether or not you're an accredited investor.

As a reminder, the SEC defines an accredited investor as a person with an annual income exceeding $200,000—$300,000 for joint income—for the last two years or a net worth exceeding $1 million excluding their primary residence. If you're an accredited investor, congratulations! If you're not, you will be excluded from certain types of investments, but not to worry, there are still plenty of opportunities for you.

## The Four Asset Classes

Go back to Chapter 5 and review Figures 5 and 6. Since you now have a balance sheet, you know the combined value of all your investments. Now, calculate the percentage of your portfolio in each of the following asset classes:

- Paper
- Real Assets
- Commodities
- Precious Metals

If you're like most people, your portfolio is not diversified. The majority of your portfolio is likely invested in paper assets. Do you think diversification is important? If so, a change is needed.

## Alternative and Conventional Investments

Again, go back to Chapter 5 and review Figures 5 and 6. You'll see that conventional investments fall within the paper asset class while alternatives are spread across all four asset classes. Calculate the percentage of your portfolio that is invested in conventional versus alternative investments. If you're like most people, your portfolio consists primarily of conventional investments. Do you think alternatives have numerous advantages over conventional investments? If so, a change is needed.

## Reserves

Just like having a deep pantry or an emergency kit, you need a financial emergency kit—reserves—before you make your first investment. Ergo, before you invest your next dollar, whether it be in alternatives or conventional investments, you need to make sure you have adequate cash reserves or reserves, even if it means discontinuing contributions to your IRA or 401K.

Investopedia defines cash reserves as "…the money a company or individual keeps on hand to meet short-term emergency funding needs." Other names for reserves are an emergency fund and a rainy-day fund. To be clear, this means that if you lose your job and have no other source of income, your reserves will allow you to pay all your bills for a certain period of time. More on that later.

Most Americans don't maintain cash reserves, and we saw this play out in real life during the 2020 COVID Pandemic when businesses and individuals didn't have the cash on hand to survive a few weeks, much less a few months, without a paycheck or paying customers.

The main characteristics of reserves are as follows:

- Accessible – readily available
- Liquid – readily convertible into cash
- Non-volatile – value doesn't fluctuate

For your reserves to meet the above characteristics, they need to be in cash or a cash equivalent like a savings account, money market fund, or certificate of deposit. I hold my reserves in a specific type of cash value life insurance policy. Here my reserves are accessible, liquid, non-volatile, and the insurance policy has the added benefit of paying 5 percent tax-free interest and is protected from creditors. See Blog #36 and #37 at TheProlificInvestor.net to learn about these policies.

How large your reserves need to be depends on your personal circumstances. If you are an employee who receives a regular paycheck, three-to-six months is a good target. If you get paid on commission, and those paychecks are irregular, twelve months might be more appropriate.

Some of you might be tempted to do what I'm about to describe, so let me stop you right now. Here's what not to do; look at your stock market portfolio and earmark some portion of it as reserves. Why? Think about what sometimes precedes a personal financial crisis, a national economic crisis. At the precise time when you need to sell the portion of your portfolio that you earmarked as your reserves, your portfolio's value will likely be down, and you'll need to sell off more shares to generate the same amount of cash as you would have before the crisis. This will discourage you from selling and put you in an emotional dilemma.

I wouldn't recommend building a portfolio on one company's stock, but it makes for an easy example. Let's say prior to an economic crisis, you own 2,000 shares of the Campbell Soup Company (CBD), currently trading at $50 per share, $100K total value. In short order, the U.S. goes into a steep recession, you get laid off, and CBD's share price drops from $50 per share to $40 per share, a 20 percent drop. Now your $100,000 portfolio is only worth $80,000.

Let's also say that you previously calculated that six months' worth of reserves for you and your family equaled $30,000, so you had earmarked $30,000 of your stock portfolio as reserves. Let's look at the amount of CBD shares you'd have to sell both before and after the economic crisis to generate your $30,000 in reserves.

Before the crisis and the 20 percent decline in the stock price of CBD, you would have to sell 600 shares to generate your $30,000 of cash reserves. After the crisis and stock decline, you'd have to sell 750 shares to generate the same $30,000 in reserves. Remember the old adage of buying low and selling high? In this example, you did just the opposite—sold low. You would have been much better off having your reserves in cash and picking up additional shares of CBD, buying low, as your financial situation improved.

| | Before Crisis | After Crisis |
|---|---|---|
| CBD Share Price | $50 | $40 |
| # Shares | 2000 | 2000 |
| Portfolio Value | $100,000 | $80,000 |
| Reserves Earmarked | $30,000 | $30,000 |
| Reserves % of Portfolio | 30.00% | 37.50% |
| Shares Needed to Generate $30K | 600 | 750 |
| Remaining Portfolio Value | $70,000 | $50,000 |

**Figure 15: How Not to Hold Reserves**

Having accessible, liquid, and non-volatile cash reserves give you and your family great peace of mind and flexibility. When the next hardship comes, and it will come in some form or another, you will not have the added burden of worrying about how you will pay your bills and being on the street because you got evicted or foreclosed upon. DO NOT SKIP THIS STEP!

## Financial Education—Books

It's no coincidence that financial education is the first benefit of alternative investments discussed in Chapter 5 and listed on the Hierarchy of Investors. It's one of the biggest things that differentiates alternative investors from conventional ones. To that end, the first investment you're going to make on this climb up the hierarchy is not what you might think. It's not any of the assets on the pyramid. Your first investment will be in yourself—your most valuable asset—by pursuing broader financial education.

Some foundational books are a great place to start. The problem is that the number of books from which to choose is endless, and every investor has a different list that he would recommend. All I can do is share my list with you, and as you continue what I hope will be a lifelong journey of continuing education, you will undoubtedly build your list that you will recommend to others someday. Read the following:

- *Rich Dad Poor Dad: What the Rich Teach Their Kids About Money That the Poor and Middle Class Do Not!* by Robert Kiyosaki
- *Rich Dad's CASHFLOW Quadrant: Rich Dad's Guide to Financial Freedom* by Robert Kiyosaki
- *Start Your Own Corporation: Why the Rich Own Their*

*Own Companies and Everyone Else Works for Them* by Garrett Sutton

- *Tax-Free Wealth: How to Build Massive Wealth by Permanently Lowering Your Taxes* by Tom Wheelwright
- *401(k)aos: How Our Dream of Retirement Became a Nightmare of Chaos* by Andy Tanner

## Financial Education—Podcasts

In 2013, a fellow real estate investor and I were driving around looking at properties, and he said to me, "You should listen to the Real Estate Guys Podcast."

I said, "What's a podcast?" From that day forward, I became a huge fan and consumer of podcast content.

I believe podcasts, the first of which aired in 2003, are one of the most beneficial services made possible by the information age. Now, during the formerly unproductive time of showering and shaving, eating breakfast, commuting to and from work, or driving on a boring stretch of North Dakota highway, you can learn a new language, keep up with your favorite sports team, find out what's happening in the world, be entertained, and yes, increase your financial education.

Like with books, the number of podcasts from which to choose is endless, and every investor has a different list that she would recommend. Here's my starting list for your consideration.

- The Real Estate Guys Radio with Robert Helms and Russell Gray
- Wealth Formula Podcast with Buck Joffrey
- The Wealthability Show with Tom Wheelwright
- The Rich Dad Radio Show with Robert Kiyosaki
- Passive Real Estate Investing with Marco Santarelli
- The Real Estate Espresso Podcast with Victor Menasce

## Financial Education—Seminars, Conferences, Classes

As you listen to podcasts, you will learn of seminars, conferences, and classes on various aspects of investing. Some will be online, and some will be in person. Pick what interests you and start attending these regularly—two to four per year. And yes, travel to another state if that's what it takes. Yes, these will cost you money, spend it! The best investment you can make is in your education.

Jim Rohn is well known for saying, "You are the average of the five people you spend the most time with." By attending these events, you will make new friends and colleagues, and the average income of the people you hang out with will rise, and so will your income if you take effective action.

Some of these people will be experts in the type of asset in which you eventually invest, and now you'll know someone personally whom you can call or email with questions.

## What Type of Alternative Investments Interest You?

By reading books, listening to podcasts, and attending seminars, you will gain exposure to numerous alternative investments. Which alternative investments interest you? Are you interested in notes, residential real estate, apartments, commercial real estate, precious metals, cryptocurrency, private lending, precious metals, small businesses, cash value life insurance, syndications, or something else altogether?

Once you've narrowed down your focus to a few specific assets, write them down. Read books, listen to podcasts, and attend seminars and classes specific to those assets, thus further increasing your financial education relative to those specific investments. We'll revisit this list of assets later.

## What Type of Investor Are You?

Once you've identified some specific assets, you need to ask yourself some tough questions and learn a little about yourself because this will help drive which assets you invest in or perhaps how you invest in them. Which of the following statements apply to you?

Investor #1 - I want to be involved in every aspect of my investments.

Investor #2 - I only want to be involved in the big decisions and leave the details to others.

Investor #3 - I want to be completely passive and let someone else manage everything.

If you're investor #1, you're an *active* investor. If you owned an SFR, for example, you'd want to be the property manager, the handyman, and the bookkeeper. You're happy to do everything your skill sets will allow and spend your free time managing your investment to maximize returns.

If you're investor #2, you want to be less involved than investor #1, but you'd make all significant decisions. If you had an SFR, you'd hire a property manager, handyman, and bookkeeper, but you'd oversee their work, its quality, and cost. You'd decide the appropriate rent for the unit, marketing strategy, and rental criteria. You're happy to hire out most of the work to others as long as you retain overall control.

If you're investor #3, you're a *passive* investor. You want to hand your money over to an expert who will handle all aspects of the investment. You might join a partnership where you provide the money, and your partner is investor #1, who takes care of everything else. I'm primarily a passive investor and invest in several different assets through limited partnerships where I provide the money and nothing else.

**What Do You Want from Your Investments— Investment Criteria**

I know these sound like strange questions, but "What do you want from your investments? What do you want them to do for you?"

Here are some possible answers:

- Cash Flow
- Appreciation
- Tax Advantages
- Liquidity
- Diversification

- A Certain ROI
- Control
- Asset Protection
- Insurability
- Less Volatility
- The Ability to Use Leverage

When you can articulate the answers to the above questions, you now have an investment criteria or philosophy. Trust me; this will make your life far easier in the future.

Once you've built a network of investors and experts, you will be what we call in the *deal flow*. You'll have more deals coming across your desk than you have money, and you'll be tempted to invest or chase after every one of them because they're all interesting—the shiny object syndrome.

This is when you come back to your written investment philosophy and see how the latest shiny object, also known as an investment, measures up to what you said you wanted from your investments. I've lined out my investment philosophy below.

I invest in assets that have the following characteristics:

- Appreciation
- 15% minimum annual ROI

- Built-in tax advantage—depreciation
- The ability to use leverage—banks will loan against this asset
- Return of capital within three years

Let's take four assets, mutual funds, cryptocurrency, SFRs, and apartment syndications, and see how each measures up against my criteria:

|  | Mutual Funds | Crypto -currency | SFR | Apartment Syndication |
|---|---|---|---|---|
| Appreciation | Yes | Maybe | Yes | Yes |
| 15% min ROI | No | Maybe | Yes | Yes |
| Tax Advantage | No | No | Yes | Yes |
| Leverage | No | No | Yes | Yes |
| Return of Capital - 3 Years | No | No | Maybe | Yes |

**Figure 16: Investment Criteria Example**

As you can see, only the apartment syndications get the green light across all of my criteria. The yes, no, and maybe decisions on the above items are somewhat subjective, and that's ok.

For example, I don't think mutual funds will consistently generate a 15 percent annual return; others might disagree. Will cryptocurrency appreciate? I tend to believe it will, but it could also crash and burn; we've seen it happen before.

The bottom line is to have some rules against which you choose your investments. These are my criteria and my evaluation against each investment.

Given the above, you'd think that apartments are the only assets in which I invest. Not true. There is another part of my investment philosophy, which allows for some exceptions. Sometimes, I invest in specific assets for very particular reasons. The exceptions that permit these investments are as follows:

- Tax Problem – If I know I will have a big tax bill in a particular year, I may choose to make a specific investment that will mitigate that tax bill. This might include an energy investment or an asset that receives bonus depreciation. See Blogs #29, 28, and #6 to learn about investments I made for this specific purpose.

- Lifestyle – If I love Maui, Hawaii, and plan to spend a portion of every year there, I might choose to purchase a condo in Maui to utilize three months of the year and rent it out the other nine.

- Asymmetric Returns or Asymmetric Risk/Reward Profile – This type of investment is where the upside potential is exponentially greater than the downside loss. Think of this as swinging for the fences, the grand slam. I believe in having a small portion of my portfolio in these types of investments.

Bitcoin (BTC) is probably the most current and recognizable example of an asymmetric risk/reward profile. When Bitcoin was launched in 2010, its value was less than a penny. In 2011, its price hit $1.00. To make the math easy, let's use $1.00 per BTC as our starting point. If you bought 1,000 BTC in 2010 for $1,000 and held it until 2021, when BTC hit $45,000, your $1,000 investment would be worth $45 million. Your downside was your initial $1,000 investment, while your upside was, well, *enormous*.

### Re-evaluation

Now that you've decided what kind of investor you are and what you want from your investments, review your list of alternative investments and cross off the ones that don't fall within the bounds of *the type of investor you are* and *what you want from your investments*.

It's just about time to look for the alternative investment you want to invest in and pull the trigger—a couple more steps.

## Do You Want a Business Structure?

From the financial education you've acquired to date, you know you can't get the best tax treatment and asset protection without a business structure. The question is, how seriously do you want to be about this? Do you want to maximize your investment dollars fully or not?

There's no value judgment here; it's just a question you have to answer as there are work and expenses involved in this step. You can undoubtedly begin investing in alternatives now in your name and switch to a business structure later if you choose.

Setting up a business structure will require professional assistance. Here are two resources with which you can consult.

- Anderson Business, Legal & Tax Advisors https://andersonadvisors.com/
- Corporate Direct https://corporatedirect.com/

Other advisors, you will need:

- Bookkeeper
- CPA/Tax Preparer/Advisor
- Banker

## Invest

Now go invest!

I know what you're thinking. Is this it? Is this all there is? Where is the list of assets in which I should invest that will move me to the next level?

Unfortunately, there is no such list. But after reading this chapter and diligently completing all the steps, you will already have your own list. Now it's just a matter of doing the necessary due diligence before investing.

As you've seen, most of this chapter isn't about investing; it's about gaining financial education and changing the way you think about investing, personal finance, and money in preparation for investing in alternatives.

There's no magic pill. I can't tell you what to invest in; only you can decide what's right for you. However, you've got the education, mindset, resources, and network to enable you to start looking at and evaluating assets. Go forth, have fun, and prosper!

# Continue Learning and Make a Ton of Money!

Don't forget to download the free action guide, which will help you work through the items in this chapter. Enter the URL below into your browser and enter the password to download your free action guide.

http://theprolificinvestor.net/action-guide/

Password: Ca$hflow

**Please Leave a Review!**

And finally, please leave an honest review of this book on Amazon. These reviews are critical in generating consistent book sales, which gets more people off their A$$ and managing their money with alternative investments.

THE
**Prolific**Inve$tor

Challenging Conventional Wisdom®

www.ingramcontent.com/pod-product-compliance
Lightning Source LLC
Chambersburg PA
CBHW060618200326
41521CB00007B/801